WITHDRAWN

BLACK HOLES

ENERGY

GALAXIES

GRAVITY

LIGHT

MYSTERIES OF
THE UNIVERSE

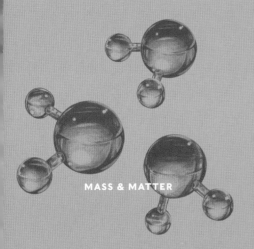

MASS & MATTER

SPACE & TIME

STARS

MYSTERIES OF THE UNIVERSE

Mass & Matter

JIM WHITING

CREATIVE
PAPERBACKS

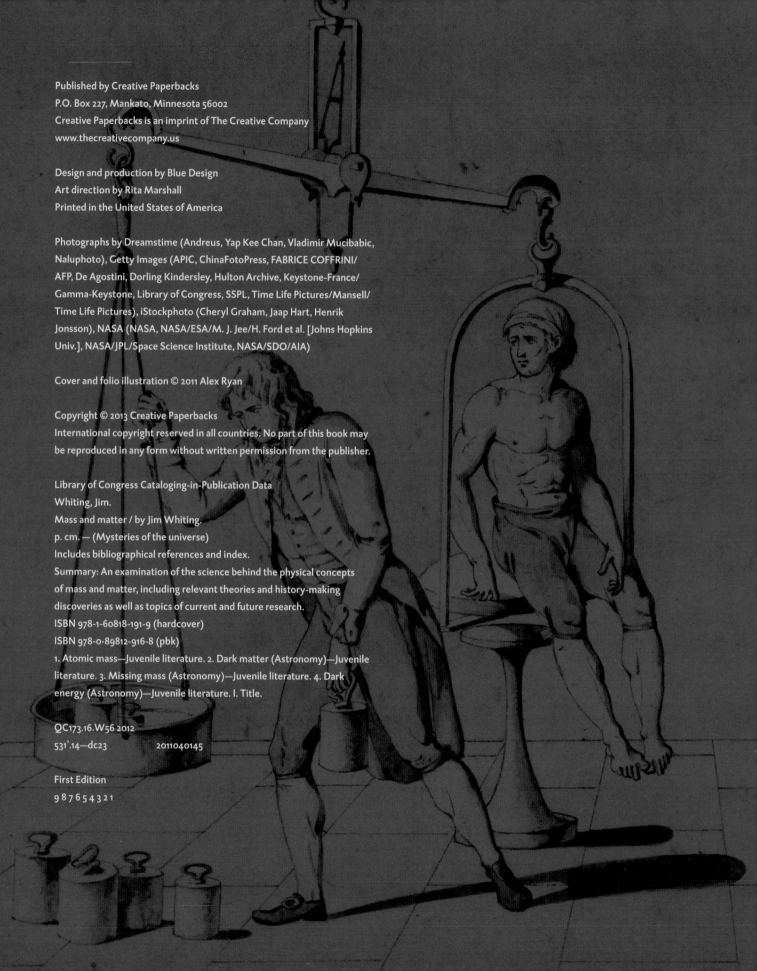

Published by Creative Paperbacks
P.O. Box 227, Mankato, Minnesota 56002
Creative Paperbacks is an imprint of The Creative Company
www.thecreativecompany.us

Design and production by Blue Design
Art direction by Rita Marshall
Printed in the United States of America

Photographs by Dreamstime (Andreus, Yap Kee Chan, Vladimir Mucibabic,
Naluphoto), Getty Images (APIC, ChinaFotoPress, FABRICE COFFRINI/
AFP, De Agostini, Dorling Kindersley, Hulton Archive, Keystone-France/
Gamma-Keystone, Library of Congress, SSPL, Time Life Pictures/Mansell/
Time Life Pictures), iStockphoto (Cheryl Graham, Jaap Hart, Henrik
Jonsson), NASA (NASA, NASA/ESA/M. J. Jee/H. Ford et al. [Johns Hopkins
Univ.], NASA/JPL/Space Science Institute, NASA/SDO/AIA)

Cover and folio illustration © 2011 Alex Ryan

Library of Congress Cataloging-in-Publication Data
Whiting, Jim.
Mass and matter / by Jim Whiting.
p. cm. — (Mysteries of the universe)
Includes bibliographical references and index.
Summary: An examination of the science behind the physical concepts
of mass and matter, including relevant theories and history-making
discoveries as well as topics of current and future research.
ISBN 978-1-60818-191-9 (hardcover)
ISBN 978-0-89812-916-8 (pbk)
1. Atomic mass—Juvenile literature. 2. Dark matter (Astronomy)—Juvenile
literature. 3. Missing mass (Astronomy)—Juvenile literature. 4. Dark
energy (Astronomy)—Juvenile literature. I. Title.

QC173.16.W56 2012
531'.14—dc23   2011040145

First Edition
9 8 7 6 5 4 3 2 1

British physicist James Chadwick,
discoverer of the neutron

TABLE OF CONTENTS

INTRODUCTION 9

CHAPTERS

MATTER MATTERS 10

THE STRUCTURE OF THINGS .17

REVIVING THE ATOM 29

ANTIMATTER AND DARK MATTER 37

MATTER ASIDES

MEASURING EARTH'S MASS .21

BLOWING UP THE VATICAN 27

DEALING WITH DARK MATTERS 41

AROUND AND AROUND WE GO 44

ENDNOTES 46

WEB SITES 47

SELECTED BIBLIOGRAPHY 47

INDEX 48

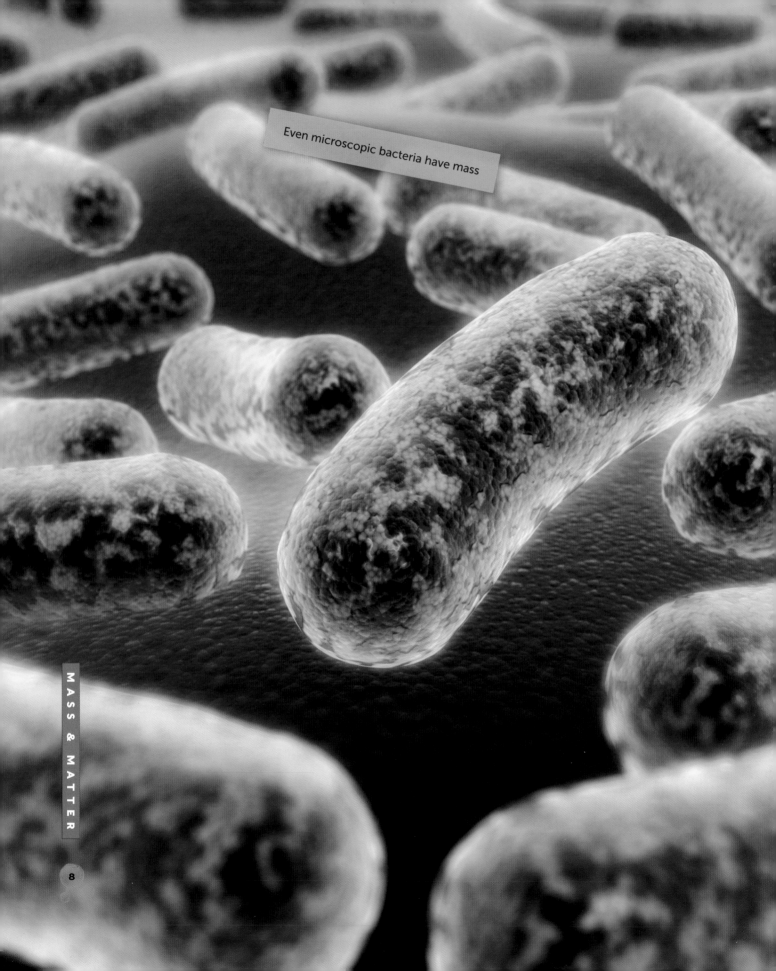
Even microscopic bacteria have mass

INTRODUCTION

For most of human history, the true nature of the universe was shrouded in myth and mystery. About 400 years ago, scientists began unraveling those mysteries. Their efforts were so successful that American physicist Albert Michelson wrote in 1894, "The more important fundamental laws and facts of physical science have all been discovered, and these are now so firmly established that the possibility of their ever being supplemented in consequence of new discoveries is exceedingly remote." William Thomson, Baron Kelvin, perhaps that era's most famous physicist, echoed Michelson: "There is nothing new to be discovered in physics now. All that remains is more and more precise measurement." Both men were wrong. Within a few years, scientists had revealed the makeup of the tiny atom and the unexpected vastness of outer space. Yet the universe doesn't yield its mysteries easily, and much remains to be discovered.

The study of mass and matter deals with everything we can detect with our senses—people, places, things, and even the air we breathe. The root "mass" forms words such as "massive" (something huge) and "massif" (a large mountain range). Yet an object's actual mass is composed of incredibly tiny things that we can't even begin to see with a microscope. This fact poses difficult questions. The first is how something so small can make things that are so large. The second is what do these "large things"—these different forms of matter—have in common? Thirdly, how are they different?

Baron Kelvin was also an engineer and mathematician

MATTER MATTERS

What do you have in common with a dog, a cat, a cactus, the moon, an artichoke, blood, an ice cube, and a maple tree? You and these objects are all made of matter. Because you're made of matter, you—and these other forms—have mass. Mass is the amount of matter an object contains. The greater the mass of something, the more matter it has. A grownup person has more mass than an infant, a tree has more mass than a twig, a bowling ball has more mass than a baseball, and so on.

Some people think of mass and weight as the same thing. They aren't. Weight measures how strongly **gravity** pulls you toward the center of the earth or of some other body. If you weigh 150 pounds (68 kg) on Earth, for example, you'd tip the scales at 25 pounds (11.3 kg) on the moon, because gravity is just one-sixth as much on the moon as it is on Earth. Gravity is directly related to mass. It's also **inversely** related to the distance from the center of an object to its perimeter, or edge. Climbers at the summit of Mount Everest, the world's highest peak, weigh a tiny bit less there. That's because they are about six miles (9.7 km) farther from the center of the earth than they are at sea level.

You'd weigh quite a bit more on the planet Jupiter. Its mass is 318 times greater than Earth's, while its diameter is 11 times longer. As a result, a 150-pound (68 kg) person would weigh 354 pounds (160.6 kg) there. Saturn presents an even more interesting situation. Its mass is 95 times greater than Earth's, while its diameter is about 9.4 times longer. Our example person's Saturn weight would therefore be just 160 pounds (72.6 kg), even though it's the second-largest planet in the solar system. On the other hand, if you're in outer space—where there is no gravity—your weight would drop to zero. Yet no matter where you travel in space, your mass remains the same.

There's another interesting aspect to weight and mass. You might think that if you

Mt. Everest is part of the Great Himalayan Range, the world's highest mountain range

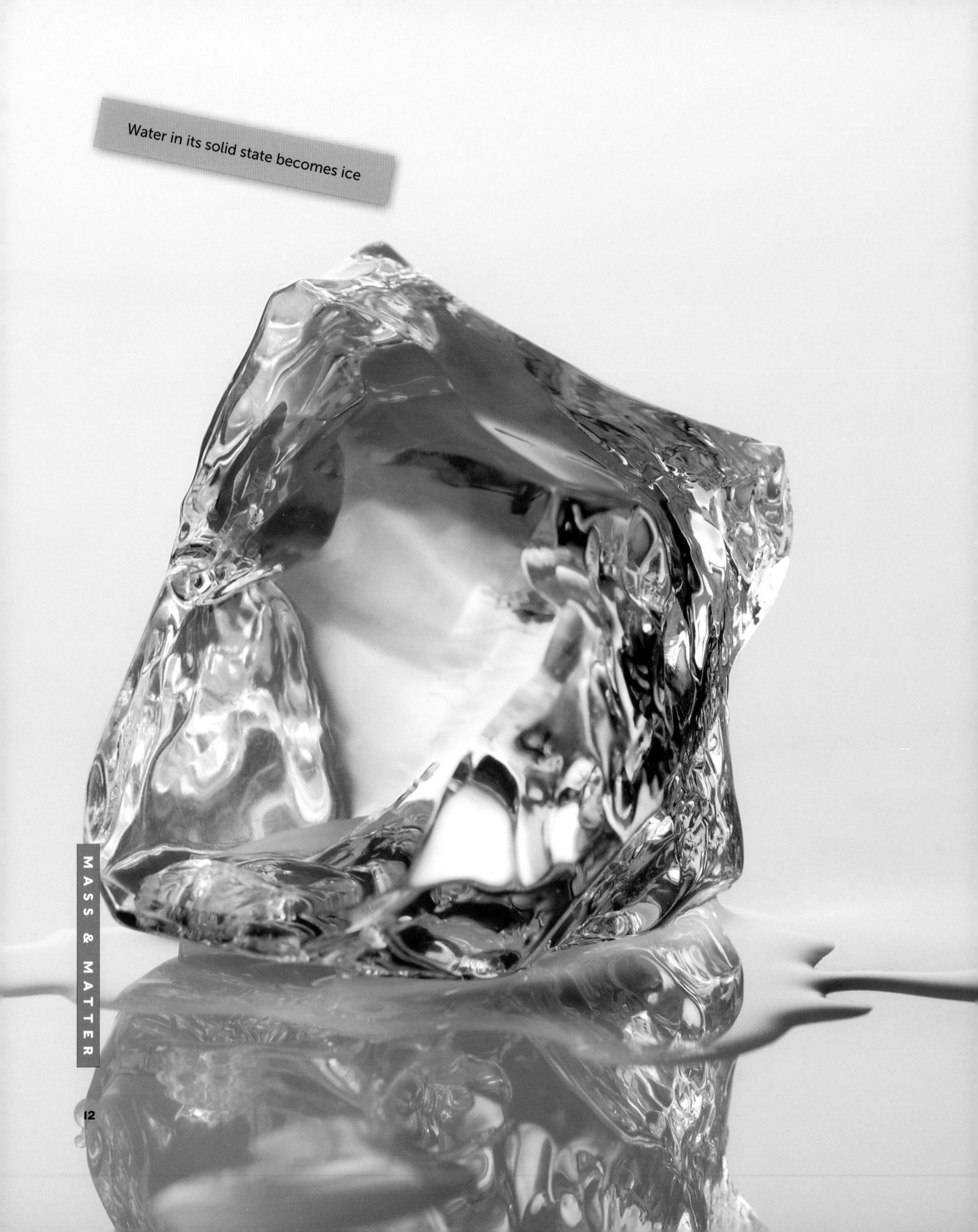
Water in its solid state becomes ice

jumped off a high diving board and dropped a golf ball at the same time, you'd beat the ball to the water. You'd be wrong. Gravity pulls all bodies downward at the same rate of speed regardless of their mass. Of course, if you repeated the dive but substituted a feather for the golf ball, you'd probably be back on the surface and catching your breath before the feather even touched down. That's because friction, or resistance, from the air slows down the feather. If you were on the moon's surface, where there's no air and therefore no resistance, you and the feather would both touch down at the same moment.

It becomes a different story if you try to move a golf ball and an object that weighs as much as you do. A slight touch will start the golf ball rolling. That same touch won't budge the bigger object, for matter has inertia. Inertia is the resistance of something to being moved. The greater the mass of an object, the more inertia its matter contains. Therefore, you need to exert more force to make that object move.

Matter usually occurs in three states as solids, liquids, and gases. It often requires the application of some process such as temperature or pressure to change from one state to another. Water provides an illustration. In its normal state, it is a liquid. If the temperature drops below 32 °F (0 °C), water freezes and becomes a solid (ice). If water is heated to its boiling point (212 °F, or 100 °C), it becomes a vapor, or a gas.

So far this all seems pretty obvious, since matter is tangible. In most cases, you can detect matter with one or more of your five senses: You can see it, hear it, touch it, taste it, and/or smell it. Or can you? Matter is composed of tiny building blocks called atoms. Atoms are 0.000000005 inches (0.000000013 cm) wide. You could fit millions of atoms into the period at the end of this sentence. A cubic centimeter of air (about the size of a sugar cube) contains billions and billions of atoms.

Atoms form 92 different chemical elements that occur in nature. These 92 elements, in different combinations, form all the millions of different kinds of matter. The atoms that compose each element are identical, yet they are different from the atoms that

make up other elements. Atoms consist of two parts. One part is the nucleus at the atom's core. The nucleus is densely packed with protons (**particles** with a positive electrical charge) and neutrons (particles with no electrical charge). In turn, protons and neutrons are made of even smaller particles called quarks. The second part of an atom is the electron cloud that surrounds the nucleus. Electrons are much smaller than protons or neutrons and contain a negative electrical charge.

In most situations involving electrical charges, particles with the same electrical charge repel each other, and particles with opposite charges attract. Because protons all have the same electrical charge, they should repel each other. But they don't. That's because protons and neutrons are all held together by the strong nuclear force, one of the four **fundamental forces** in the universe (the others being **electromagnetism**, the **weak nuclear force**, and gravity). As British physicist Stephen Hawking (1942–) explains, "Without the strong force, the electric repulsion between the positively charged protons would blow apart every atomic nucleus in the universe except those of hydrogen gas, whose nuclei consist of single protons. It is believed that this force is carried by a particle, called the gluon, which interacts only with itself and with the quarks."

The number of protons in an atom determines the element. For example, hydrogen has one proton, helium has two, and lithium has three. Gold has 79, lead has 82, and uranium, the heaviest natural element, has 92. Each element has a chemical symbol, and all the symbols can be found on the periodic table. This table lists all the elements in order of atomic number—or according to how many protons they have.

To produce substances, atoms combine into molecules. Molecules are the smallest units of a substance that have all the properties, or specific qualities, of that substance. Some molecules are relatively simple. A water molecule consists of two hydrogen

Two hydrogen atoms (white) plus one oxygen atom (red) make a water molecule

atoms and one oxygen atom. The chemical symbol for hydrogen is H, and the symbol for oxygen is O, so a **chemist** would write the formula for water as H_2O. Table salt molecules consist of one atom each of sodium and chlorine, which is written as NaCl.

Other molecules are more complicated because they involve more atoms. For example, one common form of sugar has the formula $C_{12}H_{22}O_{11}$. Twelve atoms of carbon combine with 22 atoms of hydrogen and 11 atoms of oxygen to form a single molecule of sugar.

Chemists often think of molecules as being more important than atoms. As American author Bill Bryson notes in his book *A Short History of Nearly Everything*, "Chemists tend to think in terms of molecules rather than elements in much the way that writers tend to think in terms of words and not letters, so it is molecules they count, and these are numerous to say the least." With all the matter that exists in the universe, there are endless combinations of atoms to go with it. And molecules are just the beginning.

Greek philosopher Democritus

THE STRUCTURE OF THINGS

Perhaps more than any other ancient civilization, the Greeks were curious about the world around them. One of their particular interests was trying to figure out what things were made of. By the sixth century B.C., Greek philosophers, or thinkers, were explaining things in terms of naturalistic solutions based on observable physical laws rather than in terms involving supernatural actions performed by gods.

Around 585 B.C., Thales of Miletus began the process by saying that all matter was based on water. By about 400 B.C., Democritus had developed a more complex theory. Picking up an object, he asked himself, "Can I cut this in half? And again? And again?" At some point, he thought he would not be able to cut the object in half anymore. He had arrived at the smallest possible particle of the object with which he had begun. He called this particle an atom, from the Greek *a-*, "not" and *tomos*, "a cutting." In other words, an atom is something indivisible. "Nothing exists except atoms and empty space; everything else is opinion," Democritus said.

Democritus's theory had competition. About half a century earlier, another Greek named Empedocles said that everything consisted of four basic elements: earth, air, fire, and water. These four elements were mixed in various proportions to create everything on Earth. The more air and fire it had, the lighter an object would be. Objects with more earth and water would be heavier. Aristotle, the most important ancient Greek thinker, adopted Empedocles's theory. He added another element called ether, of which he believed the sun, moon, planets, and stars were made.

Aristotle's beliefs dominated scientific thinking for nearly 2,000 years, and there was little progress on the elemental front. Some of the most interesting—if ultimately fruitless—"research" was carried out by alchemists. Alchemy, which dates back to at least the second century B.C., is the effort to change one type of matter into another. By about A.D. 1000, alchemists had begun to search for the "philosopher's stone," a legendary

substance that would change so-called base metals, such as lead, into precious metals, such as gold and silver. The philosopher's stone was also regarded as an **elixir** of life, conferring youthfulness and possibly even immortality on its owner. Some alchemists were sincere, hoping they could discover a process that would make themselves and others wealthy. Other alchemists were the con men of their time, swindling clients out of substantial sums of money for what they knew to be worthless formulas.

Thanks to alchemy, a previously unknown chemical element was discovered. Seventeenth-century German alchemist and merchant Hennig Brand thought that, since urine was golden in color, it must contain some actual gold. He let buckets of urine sit in direct sunlight until maggots appeared, then boiled it down into a thick syrup. He

French alchemist Nicolas Flamel

NICOLAVS FLAMELLVS,

Pontisatensis,

The oceans make up 0.02 percent of Earth's mass

Measuring Earth's Mass

...wasn't his intention, ...ntist Henry Cavendish ...ay of determining ...s with an experiment he ...to find its **density** in ...spended a wooden rod ...iling with a wire. At each ...od he placed a two- ...lead ball weighing 1.6 ...kg). Then he positioned ...s—each of which was ...cm) in diameter and ...8 pounds (158 kg)—on either side of the rod. The larger balls exerted a faint but measurable gravitational pull on the smaller ones. To eliminate the effects of wind and temperature changes, Cavendish put the apparatus in a small shed with two-foot-thick (61 cm) walls. He inserted two telescopes into the walls to observe how much the wooden rod twisted from the gravitational force the large balls exerted on the smaller ones. Later researchers used essentially the same method to figure out the mass. Since they knew the respective weights of the two balls and the gravitational pull of the earth on the small ball, they could **extrapolate** those numbers and determine the earth's mass. It comes out to 6,585,000,000,000,000,000,000 tons, or 6.585×10^{21} (5,9743,600, 000,000,000,000,000,000 kg, or 5.9736×10^{24}).

stored the syrup until it turned black, then **distilled** the black substance to produce a white paste. Although the paste didn't glitter like gold, it glowed and sometimes even spontaneously burst into flame. Brand named his new element phosphorus, which is derived from Greek words meaning "bearer of light." Today, one form of phosphorus is used in the tips of matches to ignite them and in fertilizer to promote the growth of crops. Another form is highly flammable and is used in weapons.

S tarting in the early 1600s, genuine scientific research had begun to erode what little factual basis alchemy might have had. Aristotle and his fellow Greeks had believed that they could figure things out just by thinking. They didn't perform experiments to check out their ideas. Now scientists were taking a different approach. The pace of investigation picked up in the 1700s and reached a peak early in the 19th century with the revival of the atomic theory, which harked back to Democritus while adding new information.

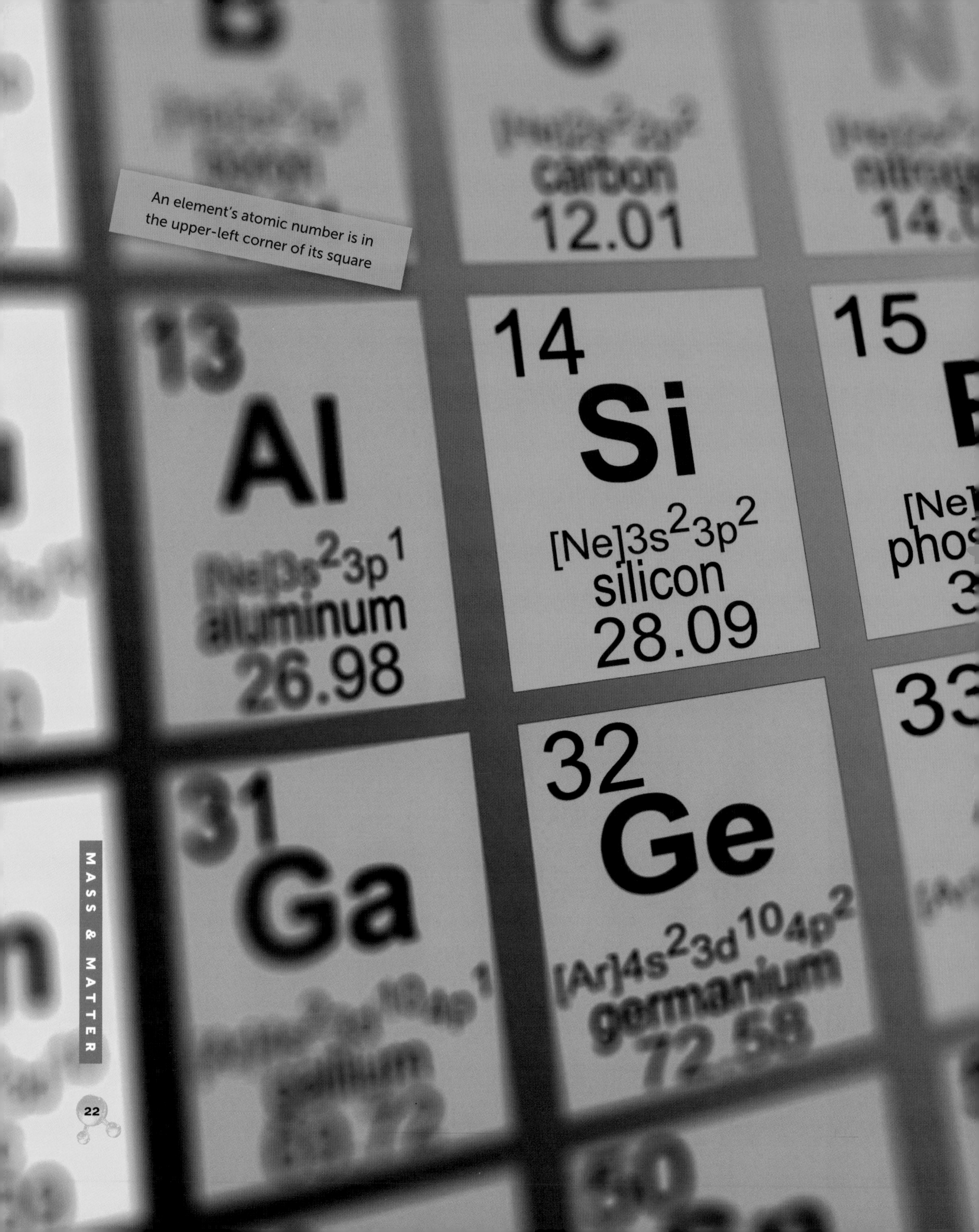

carbon
12.01

N
14.0

13
Al
[Ne]3s^{2}3p^1
aluminum
26.98

14
Si
[Ne]3s^{2}3p^2
silicon
28.09

15
P
[Ne]
phos
3

31
Ga

32
Ge
[Ar]4s^{2}3d^{10}4p^2
germanium
72.58

33

For nearly a century after its revival, the atom was regarded in its original sense, as something indivisible. An important development came in 1869, exactly 200 years after Brand's discovery of phosphorus, when Russian chemist Dmitri Mendeleev formed the periodic table of the elements. He began by writing on cards the properties of the 67 then known elements. As he laid the cards out in horizontal rows according to the elements' atomic numbers, he found that elements with similar properties were grouped in vertical columns. The table also predicted the likelihood of yet-to-be discovered elements that would follow the pattern already established by existing elements.

A flurry of findings that began at the end of the 1800s and continued well into the 1900s demonstrated that the original model and meaning of the atom was incorrect. First came the discovery of the electron as a distinct part of an atom.

Proof of the existence of further subatomic particles—protons and neutrons—soon followed. A conception of the basic structure of the atom was completed in the early 1930s, and one of the most fateful discoveries in human history came in 1938 with the knowledge that an atom could be split.

In 1905, German-born physicist Albert Einstein had shown the tremendous potential energy contained in a tiny amount of matter through his famous **equation** $E=mc^2$. In the formula, E stands for energy, m for matter, and c^2 is the speed of light (186,282 miles, or 299,792 km, per second) squared, or multiplied by itself. Scientists soon realized that splitting the atom would release this tremendous energy, and weapons of almost inconceivable destructive power could be created. With World War II about to break out, nations raced to be the first to develop such atomic weaponry. The United States won the race and dropped atomic bombs on the Japanese cities of Hiroshima and Nagasaki in August 1945. At least 100,000 people perished immediately, and many more suffered from **radiation** poisoning.

Starting in the late 1960s, the atom was divided even further. Researchers discovered that the three basic subatomic particles—protons, neutrons, and electrons—were composed of a dizzying array of even tinier particles. There are so many, in fact, that physicists refer to them as a "particle zoo." Perhaps the best known are quarks. American physicist Murray Gell-Mann (1929–), who played an important role in their discovery, named them after a seemingly nonsensical quotation from Irish novelist James Joyce's novel *Finnegan's Wake*: "Three quarks for Muster Mark." The number three is appropriate because later research revealed that protons and neutrons each contained three quarks. Quarks come in six types, or "flavors": up, down, strange, charm, top, and bottom. The first two are the most common in the universe, and because they have the lowest

Russian chemist Dmitri Mendeleev

St. Peter's Basilica in Vatican City

Physicist Murray Gell-Mann in 2010

Blowing Up the Vatican

In American author Dan Brown's 2000 novel *Angels and Demons*, members of a secret society called the Illuminati plot to blow up Italy's Vatican City—the heart of the Roman Catholic Church. They steal a canister of antimatter from the European Organization for Nuclear Research (CERN) headquarters in Switzerland, where it was manufactured, and plant it in a secret location. American university professor Robert Langdon, an expert on secret societies and their symbols, has just 24 hours to undermine the conspiracy and prevent the destruction of the Vatican. The book didn't sell many copies when it was first published. However, the overwhelming success of Brown's *The Da Vinci Code* in 2003 created considerable interest in *Angels and Demons*, and sales picked up. The book was made into a film in 2009 with Tom Hanks portraying Langdon. The popularity of the book and movie caused CERN to set up a Web site to explain the science behind antimatter. According to CERN, some "facts" about antimatter presented in the book and film aren't accurate. The main one is that, at the current rate of production, CERN would need millions of years—perhaps even billions—to make enough antimatter to fill a toy balloon. So the canister of antimatter Langdon searches for couldn't possibly exist.

masses, they are also the most stable of quarks. The other four can be created only in high-speed collisions among subatomic particles. Other subatomic particles and classes of particles boast similarly exotic names, from baryons, bosons, hadrons, and leptons to mesons, muons, neutrinos, and pions.

The ultimate construction of an atom isn't the only mystery yet to be solved about mass and matter. Today, some scientists are delving into the realm of antimatter, which takes what is known about atoms and matter and, in essence, turns it upside down. Antimatter particles are thought to act in the opposite manner to particles of matter.

While considerable atomic research takes place at ever decreasing intervals of size, other research moves in the opposite direction, toward the "big picture." Many astronomers believe that a substance called dark matter exists in the universe and has a profound effect on its future development.

Antoine Lavoisier with his wife (and fellow chemist) Marie-Anne

REVIVING THE ATOM

Some people believe that the study of matter officially became "scientific" in 1661 when English scientist Robert Boyle (1627–91) published *The Sceptical Chymist* [sic]. Boyle attacked Aristotle's theory by saying that there were more than four basic elements. He believed matter consisted of tiny particles that were identical to each other. These particles formed themselves into different combinations, which accounted for the different types of matter in existence.

Boyle distinguished between chemical mixtures and compounds. A mixture is two or more elements that can be combined but then easily separated back into their constituent elements. For example, salt water is a mixture. If a pan of salt water is left out in the sun, the water evaporates and leaves the salt behind. Compounds are unions of two or more elements that cannot be separated by physical methods such as evaporation. The only way they can be separated into their respective elements is through chemical reaction.

French scientist Antoine Lavoisier (1743–94) added to Boyle's ideas. He compiled a list of 23 elements that could not be broken down any further, though some turned out to be compounds rather than elements. Perhaps the most important aspect of his work was the formulation of the law of conservation of mass. This holds that the mass of matter remains constant over time. Even though matter can change its state in a chemical reaction, there is no gain or loss in its mass. For instance, burning a log reduces the wood to ashes. Yet its mass is still the same. Through the process of combustion, it has simply taken on different forms, such as gases and smoke.

An English chemist took the next step in our understanding of matter. In 1808, John Dalton (1766–1844) published *A New System of Chemical Philosophy*, which made him famous. In it, he revived Democritus's idea of atoms and formulated the atomic theory. It had several basic principles, which may be combined and summarized as follows:

1. All matter is composed of tiny, indivisible particles called atoms.
2. Atoms are the units of chemical changes, and they cannot be created, destroyed, or transformed into other atoms in a chemical reaction.
3. All atoms of a given element are identical, particularly in their mass. Atoms of the same element have the same mass, while atoms of different elements have different masses.
4. Atoms of different elements combine in simple, **whole-number ratios** to form compounds and can be rearranged or separated in chemical reactions.

Dalton became the first person to determine the values of "atomic weights." Since individual atoms were far too small to weigh, he constructed a table that assigned hydrogen (the lightest element) a weight of 1. The other weights were based on their relationship to hydrogen. In Dalton's system, oxygen was 7 times heavier than hydrogen, sulfur was 13 times heavier, and gold was 190 times heavier. While his calculations weren't completely accurate—modern measurements give figures of 16, 32, and 197 respectively—his atomic theory transformed scientific thinking. The atom's identity as the basic building block of matter became firmly established.

That belief lasted until nearly the end of the 1800s, when scientists began probing more deeply into the atom's structure. In an 1897 experiment, English physicist Joseph J. Thomson (1856–1940) removed the air from a sealed tube. Then he passed an electrical current through the tube onto two terminals, or connection points. The positive terminal glowed green. When Thomson moved a magnet by the terminal, the glow followed the magnet. Thomson concluded that the glow was produced by negatively charged particles he called corpuscles. Eventually, these particles became known as electrons. It was the first hint that the atom might be composed of smaller particles. Thomson tested other substances with the same results and concluded that all atoms contained electrons. They were incredibly tiny, just .0005 the size of a hydrogen atom.

ELEMENTS

		W.t			W.t
⊙	Hydrogen.	1	⊕	Strontian	46
⊖	Azote	5	✳	Barytes	68
●	Carbon	54	Ⓘ	Iron	50
○	Oxygen	7	Ⓩ	Zinc	56
◉	Phosphorus	9	Ⓒ	Copper	56
⊕	Sulphur	13	Ⓛ	Lead	90
◐	Magnesia	20	Ⓢ	Silver	190
◑	Lime	24	Ⓖ	Gold	190
	Soda			Platina	

Dalton's table used different names for a few of the elements

English physicist Joseph Thomson

A negative charge needs a corresponding positive charge for electrical balance. Therefore, Thomson's negative electron required that atoms contain something positive. He didn't know what that "something" might be. Thomson thought electrons were like tiny fruits such as currants, embedded in a much larger "bun" that somehow contained a positive charge.

That bun model of the atom didn't last long. Before it could be disproven, however, in 1905 Albert Einstein (1879–1955) created a scientific sensation with his groundbreaking equation, $E=mc^2$. Almost unnoticed in the flurry of excitement that this equation generated was another finding he released at the same time. Despite the work of Dalton, Thomson, and others, many people didn't believe that atoms existed because no one had ever seen one. In 1828, English botanist Robert Brown had described the seemingly random movement of pollen grains suspended in water—a phenomenon known as Brownian motion.

Einstein believed that millions of water molecules colliding with the grains caused the movement. He developed mathematical equations that predicted how far the grains would move and the paths they would take. When other scientists followed the equations and confirmed Einstein's thinking, no one could doubt the atom's existence.

Then, New Zealand-born physicist and chemist Ernest Rutherford (1871–1937)—a friend of Thomson's—developed the "planetary" model of the atom in a 1909 experiment. Using a special apparatus, he directed **alpha particles** at an extremely thin sheet of gold foil in a **vacuum chamber**. A **phosphorescent** screen lay behind the foil and showed the points of impact of the particles. Rutherford thought all the particles would pass through the sheet. Almost all did, but a few—perhaps 1 of every 8,000—bounced off at a 90-degree angle. A handful even came almost straight back. "It was quite the most incredible event that has ever happened to me," he wrote. "It was almost as incredible as if you fired a 15-inch shell at a piece of tissue paper and it came back and hit you."

Rutherford puzzled over what had happened for more than a year before the explanation came to him. Nearly the entire atom must be composed of empty space, with negatively charged electrons swirling around the edges and a tiny center, or nucleus, of positively charged protons. In relative terms, if an atom were the size of a cathedral, this center would be the size of a pinhead. However, the nucleus accounted for 3,999/4,000 of the total mass of the atom, and it was this nucleus that had deflected the alpha particles.

Something was still missing from that picture, though. Rutherford knew that every element's atomic number corresponded to the number of protons in its atoms' nuclei. Thus, hydrogen's atomic number was 1, helium's was 2, and so on. For relatively lightweight elements such as carbon and oxygen, the atomic weights were twice as much as the atomic number. For heavier elements, the atomic weight more than doubled the atomic number. A heavy element such as iron had an atomic number of 26, while its atomic weight was 55.

Yet the number of electrons and protons had to be equal to maintain electrical balance. Rutherford believed that there had to be a third particle, carrying no electrical charge, accompanying protons in the nucleus and weighing the same. He called it the neutron. After 10 years of painstaking work, Rutherford's former student James Chadwick (1891–1974) proved its existence in 1932. Chadwick's discovery set the stage for the splitting of the atom and the release of its incredible energy. In 1945, the world entered the atomic age, and the effects of that era continue to the present day.

Scientist Ernest Rutherford, circa 1920

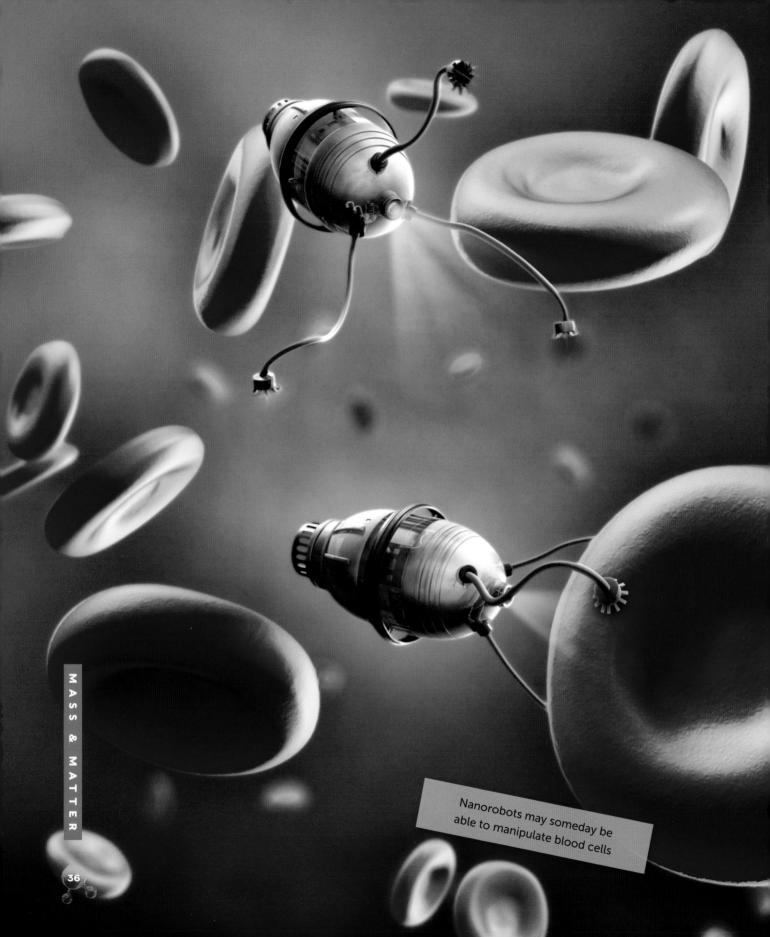

Nanorobots may someday be able to manipulate blood cells

ANTIMATTER AND DARK MATTER

The onset of the atomic age was hardly the end of research into mass and matter. It continues to occupy the attention of many scientists, and considerable contemporary research promises to provide practical applications. For example, an emerging field called nanotechnology involves working at the atomic and molecular levels to make new products, sometimes building them one atom at a time. It is based on a unit of measure called the nanometer, or one billionth of a meter.

Nanotechnology has already generated products such as sunscreens (with smaller particles that don't leave the glaring white sheen on your skin), wrinkle-resistant fabrics, self-cleaning glass, and tennis rackets lighter than steel but considerably stronger. Early in 2011, researchers Valeria Nicolosi of Britain's Oxford University and Jonathan Coleman of Ireland's Trinity College Dublin announced a new method of layering materials to make one-atom-thick nanosheets that could be used in electronic devices and as energy conductors. Such nanosheets might even power electric cars someday. Because nanoparticles are much smaller than other particles and therefore more likely to be absorbed by the body, they could present a health hazard. Further research is necessary to ensure that nanotechnology is as safe as possible.

Another future possibility related to nanotechnology is the **nanorobot**, still years away from being available for practical use. Medical researchers are particularly interested in nanorobots' potential for treating disease. Lasting for years or even decades, the microscopic robots could be inserted into the bloodstream to perform such tasks as destroying cancerous cells while leaving healthy cells alone. A team of researchers associated with the Center for Automation in Nanobiotech has discovered another use: halting possible influenza epidemics by using nanorobots to immediately sense the buildup of cells infected by the virus so treatment can begin.

Other research into matter focuses on its opposite—antimatter. In 1932, the

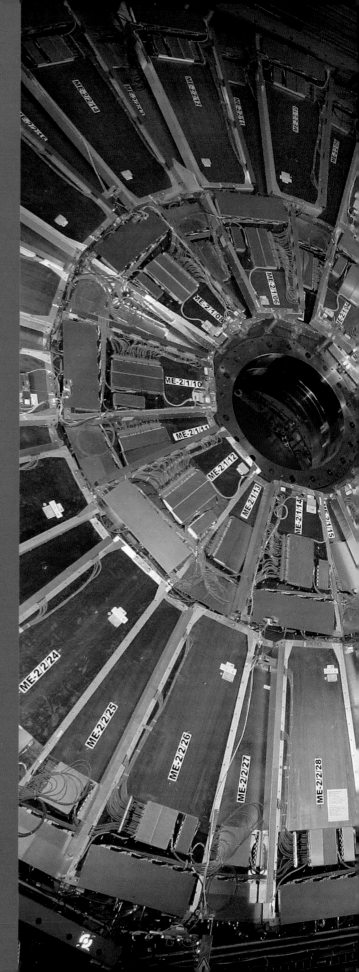

existence of antimatter was confirmed with the discovery of the positron (the positively charged equivalent of the electron). Antiprotons (the opposite of protons) were detected in 1955, an antihydrogen nucleus was created under lab conditions in 1965, and a complete antihydrogen atom followed three decades later. In 2010, scientists at the European Organization for Nuclear Research (CERN) announced they had created 38 antihydrogen atoms and kept them "alive" for a tenth of a second. They hope to build on this success.

Antimatter research may shed light on the origins of the universe. Most scientists believe that an event called the Big Bang started everything. According to this theory, the universe was created from a single dense cluster of matter about 13.7 billion years ago. In an instant, this cluster—perhaps no bigger than an atom—exploded and expanded, creating both matter and antimatter. However, the two cannot coexist. They destroy each other at the moment of contact and produce energy.

CERN uses the Large Hadron Collider to research mysteries of physics

A solar flare eruption can make looped structures called solar prominences

Dealing with Dark Matters

The 2007 film *Dark Matter* features the struggles of a brilliant Chinese graduate student named Liu Xing (played by Liu Ye) as he tries to research dark matter against the wishes of his mentor. Xing enrolls at Valley State University to work with his scientific idol, Jacob Reiser (Aidan Quinn), who is developing a model for the origins of the universe. Xing has difficulties adjusting to American collegiate life, so a wealthy patron of the university named Joanna Silver (Meryl Streep) helps him out. She can't do anything about the conflict that soon erupts when Xing disagrees with Reiser, though. Xing's belief in dark matter conflicts with Reiser's theory. Reiser then dismisses Xing from the doctoral program and takes on another Chinese student, Feng Gang (Lloyd Suh). Denied the chance to finish his degree, Xing drops out of school and takes a demeaning job selling beauty products. Finally, he determines to avenge himself. *Dark Matter* won the Alfred P. Sloan Prize at the prestigious Sundance Film Festival in 2007. The award, named for the longtime president of the General Motors Corporation, honors films that emphasize science or technology and/or feature a scientist in a lead role.

The energy potential in antimatter is one of the main reasons scientists continue to study it. In 2002, researchers at the National Aeronautics and Space Administration (NASA) found that a **solar flare** generated about one pound (.45 kg) of antimatter. They estimated that this amount would supply the energy needs of the U.S. for two days. Harnessing that energy and getting it to Earth is the main problem. If we were to produce antimatter ourselves, other problems present themselves. Currently, it costs too much and takes too much energy to produce even a small amount of antimatter.

Antimatter is already used by brain surgeons today, though. Using a technique called Positron Emission Tomography (PET), surgeons inject positrons in a fluid into the brain. The destructive contact between positrons and electrons generates **gamma rays**, which provide a picture of the brain's interior.

Dark matter is another area of exploration. Astronomers believe all the matter we can detect—stars, planets, gases, and so forth—accounts for just four percent of the universe. The remainder consists of substances that don't emit **electromagnetic radiation** and therefore can't be detected using current instrumentation. Of this

ANTIMATTER AND DARK MATTER

"missing" 96 percent, about one-fourth is dark matter, and the rest is **dark energy**.

The first evidence of dark matter appeared in the 1930s. Astronomers expected that stars farther away from the center of **spiral galaxies** would rotate more slowly than those closer to the center, in the same way that planets in the outer reaches of our solar system rotate more slowly than those closest to the sun. Yet observations that began in the 1960s revealed that they rotate at the same speed. Under normal gravitational conditions, those stars should fly apart. Because they don't, the most likely explanation is that there is something—dark matter—preventing this from happening.

Astronomers believe that dark matter may have its origin in one of two phenomena. One possibility is Massive Compact Halo Objects, or MACHOs. Somewhat mysterious in origin, these bodies may be anything that drifts through space emitting little or no visible light, from **black holes** to dim stars called brown dwarfs. MACHOs have a lensing effect on stars from distant galaxies, meaning they focus and brighten light from those stars as they move in front of them. Measuring these effects gives us clues as to the size of the MACHO.

Dark matter could also come from WIMPs (Weakly Interacting Massive Particles), which may be particles left over from the Big Bang, or byproducts of the fusion going on inside the sun and stars. WIMPs are heavier than hydrogen atoms and are capable of slicing through normal matter. They would have to exist in unimaginably large numbers to account for the abundance of dark matter in the universe. They are also much more difficult to detect than MACHOs because they don't interact with normal matter, so thus far there is no proof of their existence. "What we primarily know is what dark matter is not," explains German physicist Uwe Oberlack of the Johannes Gutenberg Universitat (Mainz), one of the world's leading authorities on the

A ring of dark matter can be superimposed on telescopic images of galaxies

Around and around We Go

The Large Hadron Collider (LHC), administered by CERN and located near Geneva, Switzerland, is one of the world's largest scientific instruments. Scientists believe the device will help answer some of the most important questions in physics, especially those dealing with subatomic particles. The LHC is a circular system of tubing about 17 miles (27 km) around, buried 328 feet (100 m) underground. Two particle beams, each containing trillions of protons, zoom around the ring in opposite directions at a rate of 11,245 times a second as they approach the speed of light (186,282 miles, or 299,792 km, per second). With all these particles flying around, collisions are inevitable, and more than 600 million happen every second. The impetus for this mind-boggling speed comes from strong magnetic fields generated by 9,300 magnets. The magnets are chilled to -458.9 °F (271 °C) using a system of liquid helium. That's less than a degree above absolute zero. To analyze the massive amounts of data the LHC will produce, tens of thousands of computers around the globe are connected in a network called the Grid. CERN officials say it is the most powerful supercomputer system in the world.

subject. "Dark matter is not just transparent, but is also completely different from all other forms of material that we know."

One type of WIMP that could give scientists clues as to the nature of dark matter is called the neutralino. If it does exist, it would be between 5 and 500 times the mass of a proton. Oberlack is affiliated with one of the institutions actively involved in the search for neutralinos, the Laboratori Nazionali del Gran Sasso in Italy. Its XENON100 experiment is conducted underground to avoid the possibility of background cosmic radiation, with a xenon detector using liquid xenon cooled to -139 °F (-95 °C).

The amount of dark matter may eventually influence the fate of the universe. Astronomers currently believe that it is expanding. If there's not enough mass—the combination of normal matter and dark matter—the pull of gravity won't be strong enough to halt the expansion. It will continue on its outward journey forever. If there's too much mass, eventually it will begin contracting and collapse in on itself. The third possibility is that mass is balanced, and gravity will halt the expansion at some point, millions or even billions of years in the future.

CERN scientists at the LHC control center

One thing is certain: we will be long gone by then. In the meantime, the contributions of countless people—professional scientists and amateurs alike—have given us a clearer understanding of what we and our environment are made of. Doubtless the coming years will only contribute to this understanding, with further advances that range from the microscopic to the seemingly limitless.

ANTIMATTER AND DARK MATTER

ENDNOTES

absolute zero — the theoretically lowest possible temperature in the universe, equivalent to -459.67 °F (-273.15 °C)

alpha particles — particles consisting of two protons and two neutrons bound together into something that looks like a helium nucleus

atom — the smallest part of an element with the chemical properties of that element

black holes — areas of space with a gravitational pull so intense that not even light can escape

chemist — a person who studies the composition, structure, and reactions of matter

constituent — serving as part of a greater entity

dark energy — a mysterious force that acts opposite to gravity and pushes the universe outward

density — the mass per unit volume measured in a substance

distilled — to have heated a liquid to produce vapors, then cooled the vapors into a purified liquid form

electromagnetic radiation — radiation of electromagnetic waves, including radio waves, light waves, gamma rays, and more

electromagnetism — magnetism produced by an electrical current

elixir — a type of sweetened medicine; historically, a substance believed to prolong life indefinitely

equation — a mathematical statement which says that two quantities are equal

extrapolate — to apply results from specific situations to arrive at a more general conclusion

fundamental forces — the primary ways in which the simplest particles in the universe interact with one another

gamma rays — the shortest waves on the electromagnetic spectrum; they can be generated by radioactive materials and nuclear explosions

gravity — the force of attraction between all masses in the universe that causes objects to fall toward the center of the earth, and which keeps the moon in steady orbit around Earth and the planets in orbit around the sun

inversely — reversed in order or nature

nanorobot — a microscopic, self-propelled robot designed to perform specific tasks repeatedly and with precision on a scale of a few nanometers

particles — the smallest pieces or traces of something

patron — a person who supports an institution such as a college or arts group, usually by giving money to it

phosphorescent — emitting light without generating any heat

physicist — a person who studies matter and motion through space and time in an effort to discover the physical laws of the universe

radiation — the giving off of energy as electromagnetic waves or as particles smaller than atoms

solar flare — an eruption of magnetic energy on or near the sun's surface

spiral galaxies — galaxies structured like a spiral; arms with younger stars spiral outward from the center, where older stars are located

vacuum chamber — an enclosure from which air and other gases have been removed

weak nuclear force — a natural force that causes radioactive decay of certain elements

whole-number ratios — relationships between two or more quantities of nonfractional numbers such as 0, 1, 2, 3, etc.

WEB SITES

Ask an Astrophysicist: Dark Matter & Dark Energy
http://imagine.gsfc.nasa.gov/docs/ask_astro/dark_matter.html
Get all your "darkest" questions answered here, and find new resources for further research.

Solar System Exploration: Your Weight in Space
http://solarsystem.nasa.gov/external/weight.cfm
Discover how much you would weigh at various points throughout the solar system.

SELECTED BIBLIOGRAPHY

Baker, Joanne. *50 Physics Ideas You Really Need to Know*. London: Quercus Publishing, 2007.

Bryson, Bill. *A Short History of Nearly Everything*. New York: Broadway Books, 2003.

CERN: The European Organization for Nuclear Research. "Homepage." http://public.web.cern.ch/public/.

Chown, Marcus. *The Matchbox That Ate a Forty-Ton Truck: What Everyday Things Tell Us about the Universe*. New York: Faber & Faber, 2010.

Cooper, Christopher. *Eyewitness Science: Matter*. New York: DK Publishing, 1999.

Couper, Heather, and Nigel Henbest. *The Encyclopedia of Space*. London: Dorling Kindersley, 2009.

Hawking, Stephen, with Leonard Mlodinow. *A Briefer History of Time*. New York: Bantam Books, 2005.

Reeves, Richard. *A Force of Nature: The Frontier Genius of Ernest Rutherford*. New York: W. W. Norton, 2008.

INDEX

alchemists 17–18, 21
  search for philosopher's stone
    17–18
antimatter 27, 37–38, 41
  antiprotons 38
  positrons 38, 41
  and solar flares 41
Aristotle 17, 21, 29
astronomers 27, 41, 42, 44
atomic age 34, 37
atomic numbers 14, 23, 34
atomic weights 30, 34
atoms 13, 14, 15, 17, 23, 24, 27, 29, 30,
    33, 34, 38, 41, 44
  combining to form molecules 14,
    15, 33
  electrons 14, 23, 30, 34, 38, 41
  neutrons 14, 24, 34
  nucleus 14, 34, 38
  other subatomic particles 24,
    27, 44
  protons 14, 24, 33, 34, 38, 44
  quarks 14, 24, 27
  splitting 24, 34
Big Bang 38, 42
black holes 42
Boyle, Robert 29
  The Sceptical Chymist 29
Brand, Hennig 18, 21, 23
Brown, Dan 27
  Angels and Demons 27
Brownian motion 33
Bryson, Bill 15
  A Short History of Nearly
    Everything 15
Cavendish, Henry 21
CERN 27, 38, 44
  Grid supercomputer system 44
  Large Hadron Collider 44
Chadwick, James 34
chemical compounds and mixtures
    29, 30
chemical elements 13, 14, 15, 18, 21,
    23, 29, 30, 34, 42, 44
  carbon 15, 34

chlorine 15
gold 14, 18, 30
helium 14, 34, 44
hydrogen 14, 15, 30, 34, 42
iron 34
lead 14, 18
oxygen 15, 30, 34
phosphorus 21, 23
silver 18
sodium 15
sulfur 30
uranium 14
chemical symbols 14, 15
chemists 15, 29, 33
Coleman, Jonathan 37
Dalton, John 29–30, 33
  A New System of Chemical
    Philosophy 29
  table of atomic weights 30
Dark Matter (film) 41
Democritus 17, 21, 29
Einstein, Albert 24, 33
  $E=mc^2$ equation 24, 33
electromagnetic radiation 41
Empedocles 17
energy 24, 38, 41, 42
  dark energy 42
expanding universe 44
five senses 9, 13
four basic elements 17, 29
fundamental forces 14
galaxies 42
Gell-Mann, Murray 24
gravity 10, 13, 14, 21, 42, 44
  relationship with mass 10, 13, 21
  and weight 10, 21
Hanks, Tom 27
Hawking, Stephen 14
Kelvin, William Thomson, 1st Baron
    9
Laboratori Nazionali del Gran Sasso
    44
Lavoisier, Antoine 29
  law of conservation of mass 29
light 24, 42, 44

  speed of 24, 44
mass 9, 10, 21, 24, 29, 30, 34, 44
  of atoms 29, 30, 34
  definition of 10
  of Earth 21
  of quarks 24
Massive Compact Halo Objects
    (MACHOs) 42
matter 9, 10, 13, 15, 24, 27, 29, 30, 38,
    41, 42, 44
  and the Big Bang 38
  in chemical reactions 29, 30
  dark matter 27, 41, 42, 44
  inertia 13
  relationship with mass 10
  states of 13, 29
Mendeleev, Dmitri 23
Michelson, Albert 9
microscopes 9
moon 10, 13, 17
Mount Everest 10
nanotechnology 37
  Center for Automation in
    Nanobiotech 37
NASA 41
Nicolosi, Valeria 37
Oberlack, Uwe 42, 44
periodic table of the elements 14, 23
planets 10, 17, 41, 42
Rutherford, Ernest 33–34
  planetary model of the atom 33
stars 17, 41, 42
sun 17, 42
telescopes 21
Thales of Miletus 17
Thomson, Joseph J. 30, 33
  bun model of the atom 33
Weakly Interacting Massive
    Particles (WIMPs) 42, 44
  neutralinos 44
World War II 24
  and atomic weaponry 24